The Sahabiyat

The Female Companions of the Prophet's ﷺ Era

Jameelah Jones

GW00644901

Ta-Ha Publishers Ltd.
www.taha.co.uk

Reprinted 1998, 2000, 2002

Revised Edition printed January 2006, March 2010

Published by:
Ta-Ha Publishers Ltd.
Unit 4, The Windsor Centre, Windsor Grove
London, SE27 9NT

website:http://www. taha.co.uk/
email: sales@taha.co.uk

Written by: Jameelah Jones
General Editor: Dr. Abia Afsar-Siddiqui
Edited by: Abdassamad Clarke

A catalogue record of this book is available from the British Library.

ISBN-13: 978 1 84200 074 8

Printed and Bound in England by: De-Luxe Printers Ltd.

Contents

(may Allah be pleased with them all)

Foreword

It is important to examine the lives of some of the *Sahabiyat* (female companions of the Prophet ﷺ) during the era in which Islam was emerging, to determine the breadth and depth of women's roles.

In my view, the few examples which follow are a testimony to the vibrancy and the essential spiritual quality which exists between men and women in Islam. One sees that Muslim women were able to rise to the occasion when the situation demanded it. These women were the counterparts of their men - courageous, strong, thoughtful and ready to give all for the cause of Truth.

Women usually carried water, nursed the wounded and buried the dead in times of war. However, it was not absolutely unheard of for women to go forth into battle as was the case of Umm 'Amarah, Kanza and a few others.

Muslim women also encouraged their husbands to stand up for truth against the unbelievers and invited non-

Muslim men who loved them to consider the message of Islam and enter the fold.

Thus, I would like to present to you a few stories of the early women of Islam, both for knowledge and for inspiration.

Jameelah Jones

The following salutations are used after names:

ﷺ which is the Arabic for *sallallahu alayhi wa sallam*, meaning peace and blessings of Allah be upon him. This is always said after the name of the Prophet Muhammad ﷺ.

؇ which is the Arabic for *radhiallahu anhu*, meaning may Allah be pleased with him. This is always said after the names of the Companions of the Prophet Muhammad ﷺ.

؇ which is the Arabic for *radhiallahu anha*, meaning may Allah be pleased with her. This is always said after the names of the female Companions of the Prophet Muhammad ﷺ.

Nasibah Umm'Amarah
bint Ka'b ibn 'Awf al-Ansariyah ﷺ

Umm 'Amarah was an important Companion and a great fighter for Allah's cause. She was right-acting, ardent and devoted. She strove for Allah, relying on Him alone. She converted to Islam during the early days and was present at the second pledge of Al-'Aqabah at which she swore allegiance to the Prophet ﷺ along with her first husband Zaid ibn 'Asim, who died after the Battle of Badr. They had two sons, Abdullah and Habib, who were both Companions of the Prophet.

Nasibah bint Ka'b was also present at the Battle of Uhud with her second husband, Ghaziya ibn 'Amr and her two sons. One morning, she set out with them for the battlefield to give water to the injured. Nasibah had brought a sword, a bow and a quiver of arrows as well as her water-skin and bandages. Soon after the battle had begun, she reached the place where the Prophet ﷺ had taken up his position on relatively high ground. He was with some of his closest Companions and the battle was going in the Muslims' favour.

The Muslims continued to advance until the way into the enemy camp was open. They were tempted by the booty and began to surge into the enemy camp seeking plunder. The fifty archers chosen to guard the rear of the army saw their companions taking spoils of war and felt that they would lose out. So, totally neglecting the Prophet's ﷺ command not to leave their post no matter what happened, they left their post, assuming that the battle was over. Their commander, 'Abdullah ibn Jubair, was left with only a few archers.

When the enemy realised what was happening, they set off for the post where the Muslim archers were stationed and killed the remaining few. Then the enemy cavalry attacked the unguarded ranks of the Believers. Some of the Quraysh enemy, who had begun to flee, rejoined the battle causing some Muslims to lose heart and run away. Other faithful Muslims fought on, but the tide had now turned against the Muslims.

Once Nasibah realised that the Muslims were being defeated, she joined the Prophet ﷺ with a sword, a bow and a quiver full of arrows. She began shooting arrows until they were all used up. Ibn Qami'ah, an unbeliever from one of the clans from the outskirts of Makkah, was shouting, "Where is Muhammad? May I not survive if he survives." Then Ibn Qami'ah recognised the Prophet ﷺ and struck at him. The bow was averted by Talhah, who was standing next to the Prophet ﷺ. Talhah then threw himself in the direction of the sword and the Muslims closed in around the Prophet ﷺ to protect him. Umm 'Amarah was a part of the human barrier which protected the Prophet ﷺ. Ibn Qami'ah struck her and she struck him, but he was wearing two coats of armour which protected him from her blows. However, Ibn Qami'ah struck Umm 'Amarah on her neck so severely that her wound took one year to heal.

Umm 'Amarah had the following to say about the Battle of Uhud, "The people had left the Prophet exposed and only a few, not more than ten, remained and my husband, my sons and I myself were among them. We defended him and the people were moving around in a defeated state. I did not have my shield with me. The Prophet saw a man with a shield, so he said, 'Give your shield to someone who is fighting.' So the man gave his shield to me and I used it to defend the Prophet."

So Nasibah continued fighting, treating the wounded and carrying water for them. When her son Abdullah was wounded and bleeding, she bandaged his wound and said to him, "Rise and fight the people, my son." Upon hearing this the Prophet ﷺ said, "And who is capable of bearing what you bear, Umm 'Amarah?"

The Prophet ﷺ was very pleased with Nasibah after her bravery at Uhud and he prayed to Allah to make

Nasibah and her family his companions in Paradise.

The people also thought well of Nasibah. When 'Umar ibn al-Khattab ؓ was brought some very fine silk cloth, someone suggested that he send it to Safiyah bint 'Ubaydah, the wife of Abdullah ibn 'Umar. He said, "I will send it to someone who has more right to it than Safiyah bint 'Ubaydah. I will send it to Nasibah Umm 'Amarah, for I heard the Prophet say, 'On the day of Uhud whether I looked to the right or the left, I saw Nasibah fighting round about me.'"

Nasibah also showed her bravery by being present at the Pledge of Ridwan, when the Muslims swore to stand by the Prophet ﷺ to the death.

After the death of the Prophet ﷺ, she took part in the fighting against Musaylimah, the false prophet, in Yamamah. She went to Abu Bakr ؓ, the Khalifah, to seek permission to join the expedition with Khalid ibn al-Walid against Musaylimah. Abu Bakr ؓ said, "We know your worth in war, so go out, in the name of Allah." Abu Bakr ؓ committed her to Khalid's charge and she fought bravely at Yamamah. She was wounded in eleven different places and had her hand chopped off. Her son, Habib, was also killed.

After Musaylimah had been defeated and killed and the war was over, Nasibah returned home. Khalid ibn al-

Walid came there to treat her hand with hot oil, to seal the wound and stop the bleeding. The hot oil was even more painful than having her hand cut off.

There is a story that 'Ikrimah narrated, that Nasibah went to the Prophet ﷺ and said, "I see that everything goes to men, and I do not see anything mentioned for women." Then the following verse of the Qur'an was revealed (Surah Al-Ahzab 33:35):

For Muslim men and Muslim women, for believing men and believing women, for devout men and devout women, for truthful men and truthful women, for patient men and patient women, for men and women who humble themselves, for men and women who give sadaqah, for fasting men and fasting women, for men who guard their private parts and women who guard, and for men who remember Allah much and women who remember, Allah has prepared for them forgiveness and a great reward.

Thus Nasibah Umm 'Amarah was prepared to fight and sacrifice her own life to defend that of the Prophet's ﷺ. She is a true example of bravery and devotion and her strength of faith is inspiring.

Sumayyah bint Khayyat ﷺ

Sumayyah was a truly great woman whose faith in Allah was tested to the limits of human endurance and yet remained unshakeable, as her story reveals.

She was a slave of Abu Hudhayfah of the Bani Makhzum in Makkah, while Yasir was an associate of Abu Hudhayfah. Sumayyah and Yasir were married and had two sons.

Many years later when Sumayyah and Yasir grew old and their son, 'Ammar, was a young man, the Prophet ﷺ began to teach the word of Islam. They heard the Prophet's ﷺ message, listened to the Qur'an and believed in the revelation sent to the Prophet ﷺ. To take such a stand in the early days of Islam when few believed or were willing to follow the Prophet ﷺ, shows that they had very strong Iman. In fact, Sumayyah was the seventh person to embrace Islam.

Because Sumayyah, Yasir and 'Ammar were poor and they had no tribe or family to support them or come to their aid, they were persecuted terribly by the

The Messenger of Allah ﷺ went to Umm Salamah and told her what had happened. She said to him, "If you wish them to obey you then you must leave them and not say a word to them until you have sacrificed your animal and shaved your hair."

The Prophet ﷺ followed Umm Salamah's suggestion. When the Companions saw that the Prophet ﷺ had sacrificed his animal and shaved his hair, they anxiously arose to do the same.

Umm Salamah took part in the conquest of Khaybar. She also narrated ahadith directly from the Prophet ﷺ and from Abu Salamah and Fatimah az-Zahra. She died in either 59 or 61 AH at the age of 84. Abu Hurayrah lead her funeral prayer and she was buried in al-Baqi in Madinah.

Umm Salamah migrated twice for the love of Allah. Her migration to Madinah was a particularly painful one and she endured a long separation from her husband and son. She then endured the death of her husband, but because of her patience and faith, Allah gave her the honour of being *Umm al-Mu'mineen* (the mother of the Believers) as one of the wives of the Prophet ﷺ.

Safiyyah bint Abdu'l Muttalib ؓ

Safiyyah was the aunt of the Prophet ﷺ. She and Hamzah were the children of Hala, the wife of Abdu'l-Muttalib. Hala had been Abdu'l-Muttalib's last wife and their wedding had taken place on the same day as the wedding of the Prophet's ﷺ parents.

Safiyyah was a great lady, who accepted Islam early and took the oath of allegiance to the Prophet ﷺ and then migrated to Madinah. Before Islam, she had been married to Harith ibn Harb ibn 'Umayyah. She then married Al-'Awwam ibn Khuwaylid ibn Asad, who was the brother of the Prophet's ﷺ first wife, Khadijah ؓ. By him, she had three sons, az-Zubayr, as-Sa'ib and Abdu'l-Ka'bah. Al-'Awwam died when the children were still young, leaving Safiyyah widowed. She did not marry after that.

She was present at the Battle of Uhud when the Muslims suffered defeat. At one stage in the battle, she stood up with a lance in her hand and said to the enemy, "Are you trying to defeat the Prophet?" She waved the lance in the enemies' faces. When the Prophet ﷺ saw her, he told her son, az-Zubayr, to take her back because he did not want her to see her brother, Hamzah, who had been killed in battle. Az-Zubayr told his mother that the Prophet ﷺ had ordered her to go back. She asked, "I have heard that my brother has been mutilated and that has happened for Allah's sake. Allah has fully reconciled us to what has happened. I will remain calm and patient if Allah wills."

When az-Zubayr told the Prophet ﷺ of what his mother had said, the Prophet ﷺ told him to leave her alone. So Safiyyah came and saw Hamzah and prayed over him and said, "*Inna lillah wa inna ilayhi raji'un*." She asked Allah's forgiveness for him. Then the Prophet ﷺ ordered the Muslims to bury Hamzah.

Safiyyah also took part in the Battle of Khandaq (Trench) in 5 AH. The Jews had broken their treaty with the Prophet ﷺ and had united with the non-believers of Arabia to launch an attack on Madinah. The Prophet ﷺ put his wives and womenfolk in a fortress in order to protect them while he and his Companions were defending Madinah. The fortress was guarded by Hassan ibn Thabit. One day a Jew was walking around the fortress, and by chance Safiyyah saw him and realised he was a spy, who would inform the enemy that the fortress contained only women and children and they may attack it. Safiyyah said to Hassan, "O Hassan, this Jew is going around the fortress and the Prophet and his Companions are busy, so go down and kill him." Hassan said, "May Allah forgive you, you know that I cannot be involved in this." Hassan was unable to kill the Jew perhaps because of some illness that prevented him from fighting.

When Safiyyah heard this, she got up, took a tent pole, went down to the fortress to where the Jew was, and hit him so hard that he died, in order to protect the womenfolk of the Prophet ﷺ.

Safiyyah also participated in the Battle of Khaybar.

'Umar ibn al-Khattab ﷺ allocated 6,000 dirhams, as a yearly stipend for Safiyyah during his Khilafah. She narrated ahadith from the Prophet ﷺ and others narrated from her. She was a great poetess and recited poetry on the deaths of her father and brother, Hamzah.

Safiyyah died during the Khilafah of 'Umar ﷺ in the year 26 AH, at the age of 73. 'Umar ﷺ buried her in al-Baqi in Madinah. Other reports say that she died during the Khilafah of 'Uthman ﷺ.

Ruqayyah bint Muhammad ﷺ

Ruqayyah was born almost twenty years before the Hijrah, the second daughter of Khadijah 🌸 and Prophet Muhammad ﷺ. Her sisters were Zaynab, Umm Kulthum and Fatimah. Before the advent of Islam, she was married to 'Utbah ibn Abu Lahab, one of the sons of Abu Lahab, a paternal uncle of the Prophet ﷺ. Her sister, Umm Kulthum, was also married to another son of Abu Lahab, 'Utaybah.

However, Abu Lahab and his wife were sworn enemies of Islam from the outset and Abu Lahab told his sons to divorce the daughters of the Prophet ﷺ.

Ruqayyah accepted Islam with her mother and took the oath of allegiance to the Prophet ﷺ. She then married 'Uthman ibn 'Affan in Makkah and migrated to Abyssinia and then to Madinah with him.

During the Battle of Badr, she became ill with measles and the Prophet ﷺ went to Badr and left 'Uthman 🌸 behind to tend Ruqayyah. She died while the Prophet ﷺ was at Badr, during the month of Ramadan only seventeen months after the Hijrah. She had a son called 'Abdullah, but he too died only a few years after his mother.

When Ruqayyah died, the women cried over her and 'Umar ﷺ came along and started to scold them. The Prophet ﷺ took his hand and said, "Let them cry, 'Umar. They cry and the devil screeches. What comes from the eyes and the heart is from Allah and His mercy. That which comes from the hands and tongue is from Shaytan." (Meaning that it is acceptable to feel sad and cry over someone's death but it is not allowed to beat the chest and wail or say things against Allah).

Her sister Fatimah sat on the edge of her sister's grave next to the Prophet ﷺ and started to cry. The Prophet ﷺ wiped her tears away with the edge of his robe. Anas bin Malik narrated, "We witnessed the burial of the daughter of Muhammad ﷺ and he sat by the grave and we saw tears fill his eyes."

'Uthman ﷺ subsequently married the third daughter of Khadijah ﷺ and the Prophet ﷺ, Umm Kulthum. However, she died some six years after the marriage with no children.

Asma bint Abi Bakr ﷺ

The story of Asma bint Abi Bakr is one of bravery, faith and human endeavour. She was one of the great female companions of the Prophet ﷺ. She was born some twenty-seven years before the Hijrah. Her father, Abu Bakr as-Siddiq ﷺ, was one of a kind. He was one of the vanguard of Islam, first Khalifah of the Muslims, one of the best of creation after the Prophets and the closest Companion of the Prophet Muhammad ﷺ. Qutailah bint 'Abdul-'Uzza, a Quraysh lady from the tribe of Bani 'Amir ibn Luwiyah, was Asma's mother.

Abu Bakr ﷺ was the first adult man to accept Islam. Needless to say, Asma was raised in a Muslim environment. As Abu Bakr's eldest daughter, she grew to be knowledgeable, patient and steadfast in the path of Allah. She met pure, upright Muslims, intent upon upholding true values and high morals, all around her in her father's house. Certainly, it is hardly surprising that Asma became one of the foremost figures in Islam. She accepted Islam in Makkah without hesitation. According to historians, only seventeen people preceded her in embracing Islam.

Asma was ten years older than her sister, A'ishah 🙵. Asma was known to be witty, intelligent, diplomatic, noble and had a distinctive personality. Nothing much is known about her physical appearance other than that she was tall and attractive. She married az-Zubayr ibn al-'Awwam, one of the ten Companion promised the Garden.

Asma was known as 'She of the Two Belts' due to the part she played in the emigration of the Prophet 🙼 to Madinah. When the Prophet 🙼 and Abu Bakr 🙵 hid in a cave in Mount Thawr while the unbelievers were looking for them, Asma brought food to them. Not having a strap to tie up the bundle with, she tore her belt, or girdle, in two and used one half to carry the food.

At that time, Abu Bakr 🙵 took his entire wealth with him which was approximately 5,000 or 6,000 dirhams. After Abu Bakr's flight, his father came to enquire after the family and their financial situation. He was anxious for them. He was blind. Asma took some stones, covered them with cloth and placed his hands on the bundle saying, "Feel how much he has left to take care of us." But Abu Bakr 🙵 had not left anything with them. She only wanted to reassure her grandfather about their situation.

Az-Zubayr was somewhat stern and severe with Asma, yet she bore it patiently. Once she complained to her father, and he advised her to continue to be patient, saying, "O my daughter, be patient, for if a woman is married to a good man who dies and she does not marry anyone after him, they will be joined in Paradise."

Asma was expecting a child when they emigrated to Madinah. Her son, 'Abdullah ibn az-Zubayr, was the first child born to the Muslims after their emigration to Madinah. The Companions rejoiced because the Jews of Madinah claimed to have bewitched the Muslims so that they could not have any children. Allah showed the falsity of their claims with the birth of 'Abdullah.

Asma lived a long, full life of almost a hundred years. She narrated fifty-eight ahadith from the Prophet ﷺ. She lived to see her son assume the khilafah during a particularly turbulent period in the history of the Muslims and also saw him seek and die a hero's death at the hands of Hajjaj ibn Yusuf.

Zaynab bint Muhammad ◉

Zaynab was the second child of the Prophet ◉ and Khadijah ◉. She came to marry Abu'l-'As ibn Ar-Rabi' who was the son of Hala bint Khuwaylid, Khadijah's sister. Before the revelation, Khadijah ◉ had asked the Prophet ◉ to find a wife for her nephew, who was one of the well-respected, wealthy traders of Makkah. So, the Prophet ◉ married him to his daughter, Zaynab.

When Prophethood was granted to Muhammad ◉, Khadijah ◉ and her daughters believed in him and in his message. However Abu'l-'As did not embrace Islam. The Quraysh told him to divorce Zaynab, promising him any other woman he desired. He refused, saying that he did not want any other women of Quraysh. The Prophet ◉ always used to speak warmly of Abu'l-'As due to the stand he took against the Quraysh.

Nevertheless, Islam had made a split between Zaynab and her husband; but because very little *shari'ah* had as yet been revealed, Abu'l-'As and Zaynab continued being together as Muslim wife and non-Muslim husband until after the Hijrah.

Abu'l-'As joined the expedition to Badr on the side of Quraysh and was captured by the Muslims, so he remained in Madinah. When the Makkans sent the ransom for their prisoners, Zaynab (who was still in Makkah) sent the money for Abu'l-'As and, along with it, a necklace which her mother, Khadijah &, had given her on her wedding. When the Prophet ﷺ saw this, his feelings overcame him and he said, "If you would like her to have her captive husband back and return her money to her, do so." The people at once agreed and they let him go and sent the money back.

However, the Prophet ﷺ imposed a condition on Abu'l-'As, that upon his return he should send Zaynab to Madinah. Abu'l-'As promised to honour this condition. Allah had made it clear that a Muslim woman could not be the wife of a non-Muslim man.

After Abu'l-'As returned to Makkah, he informed Zaynab of his promise to her father and they agreed that their little daughter, Umamah, should go with her. At the time, Zaynab was expecting another child. When all the preparations had been made for the journey, Abu'l-'As's brother, Kinanah, was sent as an escort. Their plans had been kept secret but they set off in broad daylight, which upset Quraysh and they decided to bring Zaynab back to Makkah. Habar ibn Al-Aswad ibn 'Abdu'l Muttalib struck at her with his spear as she sat in the camel sedan. Kinanah dismounted to protect her. Then Abu Sufyan and some others asked Kinanah to discuss the matter calmly with them. Abu Sufyan argued that it was a mistake to bring Zaynab out of Makkah publicly. He said that people would take it a sign of weakness if they allowed Zaynab to leave in broad daylight. He said that they did not want to keep her from her father, nor did they want revenge. They asked Kinanah to take her back into Makkah and, when people stopped talking about the matter, she could steal out secretly to join her father. Kinanah accepted this proposal and they all returned to Makkah. Shortly afterwards, Zaynab miscarried due to the fright caused her by Habar.

When some time had elapsed and Zaynab had recovered sufficiently, Kinanah took her and little Umamah under the cover of night and escorted them to a valley on the outskirts of Makkah. They were met by Zayd ibn Harithah who escorted them to Madinah.

Almost five months after the Battle of Khandaq (Trench), a rich caravan of Quraysh was returning on its way from Syria, and Zayd was sent to waylay it with a hundred and seventy men. Zayd and his men captured the entire caravan and most of the men were taken captive. Abu'l-'As was among them; however, he managed to escape. Nevertheless, as he passed Madinah, he was filled with the desire to see his former wife and little daughter. So he entered the city at night and somehow found the house of his former wife. It was near the time of Fajr and when Bilal made the call to prayer, Zaynab went into the mosque, leaving Abu'l-'As with Umamah. After the Prophet ﷺ said, "Allahu Akbar" and the men repeated it after him, there was a moment of silence and in this brief moment, Zaynab cried out, "O people, I give protection to Abu'l-'As." Then she too said, "Allahu Akbar" and entered into the prayer.

When the Prophet ﷺ had pronounced the final, "As-salamu alaikum", he rose and turned to face the Muslims saying, "Did you hear what I heard?" There was a general assent. He ﷺ said, "By Him in whose hand is my soul, I knew nothing of this until I heard what I heard. The least Muslim can grant protection which shall be binding on all other Muslims." Then he went to his daughter and said, "Receive him with honour, but let him not come to you as a husband, for you are not his, by law."

She told her father that Abu'l-'As was worried about the loss of the merchandise which he himself had acquired by barter on behalf of Quraysh who had entrusted their goods to him, for he was considered one of the most trustworthy men in Makkah. So the Prophet ﷺ sent word to those who had taken part in the expedition and had taken the property of Abu'l-'As, saying, "This man is related to us as you know and you have taken this property of his. If you should be so good as to return it to him, that would please me, but if you will not, it is booty which Allah has given you, so that you have the better right to it."

They said that they would give it back to him and everything was returned, without exception. They noticed that there were signs that he had thoughts of entering Islam, so one of the men said to him, "Why do you not embrace Islam and take these goods for yourself, for they are not the property of idol-worshippers?" However, Abu'l-'As answered, "It would be a bad beginning to my Islam, if I betrayed my trust."

He took the goods to Makkah and gave them to their owners. Then he returned to Madinah and entered Islam, pledging his allegiance to the Prophet ﷺ. So Zaynab was reunited with her husband and there was great rejoicing in the family of the Prophet ﷺ and throughout the city. This occurred during the seventh year of the Hijrah.

Zaynab died the next year, in the eighth year of the Hijrah. The Prophet ﷺ was with her at the end and spoke words of comfort to her. When the body had been prepared for burial, the Prophet ﷺ led the funeral prayer and prayed by her grave. He grieved deeply for her.

Hearing his wife's comforting words, Abu Talhah left, contentment and relief in his heart, to greet the Prophet ﷺ and his other guests. The Prophet ﷺ and Abu Talhah soon came back to Umm Sulaym and the Prophet ﷺ said, "Bring me what you have, Umm Sulaym." She gave him what food she had and the Prophet ﷺ prayed to Allah to bless it. Then they gave permission to the people to enter group by group until they had all eaten. Next, the Prophet ﷺ and his household ate. Yet after everyone had eaten, Umm Sulaym and Abu Talhah still had food to give to their neighbours! Allah did not disgrace Abu Talhah and Umm Sulaym and blessed their food because they were seeking His pleasure alone.

Abu Talhah and Umm Sulaym had a son together named Abu 'Umayr. One day Abu 'Umayr died. Umm Sulaym told the members of her family not to mention the death of his son to Abu Talhah until she had told him herself.

When Abu Talhah came home, Umm Sulaym gave him his evening meal. Then she dressed and perfumed herself, which she had not done before and spent the night with her husband.

Afterwards, she said, "Abu Talhah, if some people borrow something from another family and then they ask for its return, would they resist its return?" He said, "No." So she said, "I am informing you about the death of your son." He was annoyed and said, "You did not inform me until I had spent the night with you." Abu Talhah went to the Messenger of Allah ﷺ and told him what had happened. The Prophet ﷺ said, "May Allah bless both of you because of this night."

As a result, Umm Sulaym was expecting a child. Even so, she was present on the day of the Battle of Hunayn. She was very brave and carried a dagger about her waist even though she was expecting. Abu Talhah said to the Prophet ﷺ, "O Messenger of Allah, Umm Sulaym has a dagger." Umm Sulaym replied, "O Prophet, I brought this dagger so that if any idolator comes near me, I will stab him in his stomach. I will kill those who flee from you as you kill those who are fighting you, and that is what they deserve." The Prophet ﷺ said, "Umm Sulaym, surely Allah is enough."

Abu Talhah and Umm Sulaym were later accompanying the Messenger of Allah ﷺ on a journey. When the party came near Madinah, Umm Sulaym felt labour pains. Abu Talhah remained with her and the Messenger of Allah ﷺ carried on with the rest of the group. Abu Talhah said, "O Lord, You know that I love to go along with the Messenger of Allah when he goes out and enter along with him when he enters, and I have been detained as You see." In response to this Umm Sulaym said, "Abu Talhah, I do not feel (as much pain) as I was feeling before. We can go on." So they carried on, and she felt contractions as they reached Madinah and a boy was born.

One morning, soon after the birth of the baby, Umm Sulaym asked her son, Anas, to take the baby to the Prophet ﷺ. The Prophet ﷺ said, "This is perhaps the one Umm Sulaym has given birth to." Anas said, 'Yes.' The Prophet ﷺ laid the baby in his lap and asked that 'Ajwa dates of Madinah be brought. He ﷺ softened them in his mouth and when they became soft, he placed them in the baby's mouth. When the baby began to suck the dates, the Messenger of Allah ﷺ said, "See what love the Ansar have for dates." Then he wiped his face and named him 'Abdullah.

Umm Sulaym was an example of courage, faith, contentment and wisdom in all spheres, whether on the battlefield or in everyday life. The Messenger of Allah ﷺ said about her, "I entered Paradise and heard the noise of steps. I asked, 'Who is it?' They said, 'She is Ghumaysa, the daughter of Milhan, the mother of Anas ibn Malik.'"

Wives of the Prophet ﷺ
(may Allah be pleased with them all)

1. Khadijah bint Khuwaylid ibn Asad
2. Sawda bint Zam'a ibn Qays ibn 'Abdushams
3. 'A'ishah bint Abi Bakr as-Siddiq ibn Abi Quhafah
4. Hafsah bint 'Umar ibn al-Khattab
5. Zaynab bint Khuzaymah
6. Umm Salama Hind bint Abi Umayyah
7. Zaynab bint Jahsh al-Asadiyyah
8. Juwayriyyah bint al-Harith ibn Dirar
9. Umm Habibah (Ramlah bint Abi Sufyan ibn Harb)
10. Safiyyah bint Huyayy ibn Akhtab
11. Maymunah bint al-Harith
12. Maria al-Qubtiyya

Daughters of the Prophet ﷺ
(may Allah be pleased with them all)

1. Fatimah
2. Zaynab
3. Ruqayyah
4. Umm Kulthum